The Sayings

Sayings of Jane Austen
Sayings of Lord Byron
Sayings of Winston Churchill
Sayings of Disraeli
Sayings of F. Scott Fitzgerald
Sayings of Dr Johnson
Sayings of James Joyce
Sayings of John Keats
Sayings of Rudyard Kipling
Sayings of D.H. Lawrence
Sayings of Somerset Maugham
Sayings of Nietzsche
Sayings of George Orwell
Sayings of Dorothy Parker
Sayings of Ezra Pound
Sayings of Shakespeare
Sayings of Bernard Shaw
Sayings of Sydney Smith
Sayings of R.L. Stevenson
Sayings of Jonathan Swift
Sayings of Anthony Trollope
Sayings of Mark Twain
Sayings of Oscar Wilde
Sayings of W.B. Yeats
Sayings of the Bible
Sayings of the Buddha
Sayings of Jesus
Sayings of Moses
Sayings of Muhammad

The Sayings of

F. SCOTT
FITZGERALD

edited by
Robert Pearce

DUCKWORTH

First published in 1995 by
Gerald Duckworth & Co. Ltd.
The Old Piano Factory
48 Hoxton Square, London N1 6PB
Tel: 0171 729 5986
Fax: 0171 729 0015

Introduction and editorial arrangement
© 1995 by Gerald Duckworth & Co. Ltd.
Extracts from *The Letters of F. Scott Fitzgerald*
ed. Andrew Turnbull (The Bodley Head, 1964)
© The Estate of F. Scott Fitzgerald

All rights reserved. No part of this publication
may be reproduced, stored in a retrieval system, or
transmitted, in any form or by any means, electronic,
mechanical, photocopying, recording or otherwise,
without the prior permission of the publisher.

A catalogue record for this book is available
from the British Library

ISBN 0 7156 2648 5

Typeset by Ray Davies
Printed in Great Britain by
Redwood Books Ltd., Trowbridge

Contents

- 7 Introduction
- 13 The United States of America
- 15 Dreams
- 19 Intoxication
- 23 Youth, Age & Education
- 27 Success & Failure
- 31 Money
- 33 Sex & the Sexes
- 43 Hollywood
- 45 Himself
- 52 Literature & Writers
- 58 Pessimism, Madness & Despair
- 62 Maxims & Aphorisms

Introduction

F. Scott Fitzgerald was the golden boy of American literature. Born in St Paul, Minnesota, in 1896, he blazed onto the literary scene in 1920 with *This Side of Paradise*, followed two years later by *The Beautiful and Damned*. They became instant best-sellers. A few years later came *The Great Gatsby*, which, though it sold less well, was praised by critics as a truly great novel. Success came instantly. What matter, now, that he had not made the grade at Princeton football, that his unit had not served in France, or that the beautiful Zelda Sayre had refused to marry him because of his relative poverty? Such scars could be transmuted into art, while the promise of literary success led Zelda to marry him after all. Scott Fitzgerald – surely the American Dream incarnate – seemed to have been touched by the lyrical muse: he wrote a wistful and elegant poetic prose that spoke of exquisite beauty and poignant loss. Ernest Hemingway believed that his talent was 'as natural as the pattern made by the dust on a butterfly's wings'.

Fitzgerald was the poet-chronicler of the decade he described as the 'Jazz Age ... the greatest, gaudiest spree in history', the spokesman of the postwar generation. Undergraduates, he believed, looked upon him as a sort of icon. Youth was angry at the futile destruction of the war and determined to live life without inhibitions, 'all the way up'. Scott and Zelda too would drain life to the dregs, living fully, extravagantly, exquisitely, celebrating youth and intending to kill themselves to stave off the tragedy of reaching thirty years of age – but only after Scott had become the greatest American novelist.

There were two sides to the 1920s, and to Fitzgerald's account. He celebrated the decade's exuberance and high spirits, its power and idealism. Here was a generation that would not accept the life-in-death depicted by T.S. Eliot and others. His characters sought happiness freshly and fully and were open to all the romantic possibilities of life. But he cast a jaundiced, and remarkably detached, eye on the gross self-indulgence and purposeless dissipation that too often accompanied – and sometimes consumed – their quests. He castigated the futility of those who consumed without producing as thoroughly as any socialist. He was both the greatest celebrant and the sternest critic of the Jazz Age.

It is impossible to confine Fitzgerald to a single position. One critic has spoken of his 'double vision'; another has contrasted his style, which sang of hope, with his message of despair; a third has insisted that the notorious playboy was also a religious thinker. Like his narrator in *Gatsby*, Nick Carroway, Scott Fitzgerald aspired to be 'within and without, simultaneously enchanted and repelled by the inexhaustible variety of life'. But this was a infinitely delicate balancing act. He and Zelda seemed fully absorbed in the riotous living of the 1920s: Scott once jumped fully clothed into the Pulitzer Fountain on Fifth Avenue; he was arrested half a dozen times after fights; he once took the watches and jewellery off guests at a party and boiled them in tomato soup; and on another occasion he spent a pleasant half-hour with Zelda in a revolving door. They drank deep not only of life but of bootleg alcohol. Yet it was precisely because he was so much a creature of the Jazz Age that Fitzgerald could depict it so convincingly and predict so unerringly the failures and moral bankruptcies of his characters. Here was a moralist, passing stern puritanical judgements.

He was undoubtedly within the Jazz Age, and his characters were in part projections of himself. But surely he could not be fundamentally like them? For he was a dedicated novelist, looking with the detachment of an outsider, the Midwestern boy who had so strangely wandered into the world of the very rich. He had a real purpose in life and knew what he was doing, at least at first. He was living the life of an artist, gathering material for his books – a life which he believed to be as arduous as that of a soldier in war-time.

He once wrote that it is the test of a first-rate intelligence to hold two opposed ideas at the same time and still retain the ability to function. Parties were a form of suicide, but Scott was immune; excessive alcohol intake would lead to cirrhosis of the spirit if not of the liver, but not for Scott. Money corrupted, but the novelist was above such pettiness. Even so, he found it impossible to manage on 30,000 dollars a year.

The crash for the United States came in October 1929 on Wall Street. For Fitzgerald it took longer. Zelda cracked first: schizophrenia was diagnosed, and in the 1930s she was confined to an institution. Scott once said that he left his capacity for hope on the 'little roads that led to Zelda's sanatorium'. She died in a fire in 1948. Some have said that she was jealous of her husband's success and had therefore urged him to spend his time in the pursuit of pleasure rather than work. Certainly her affair with a Frenchman in 1924 was a blow from which her sensitive husband perhaps never fully recovered. His own breakdown, described powerfully and with remorseless honesty in magazine articles known as *The Crack-Up*, was milder, but in the 1930s his health was never good. He suffered from tuberculosis and had become an alcoholic. The drink had taken him. Few wanted to read the books of 'poor Scott' any more. It seemed that his talent had gone and that he was as emotionally bankrupt as some of his characters. Initially his art had imitated life, but now the roles had been devastatingly reversed. It has been said that he jumped from a prolonged adolescence into premature old age. He died in 1940 at the age of 44.

Yet at least there had been a second act for Fitzgerald. His thirties were as awful as he had feared, and yet he kept on writing. He had to, in order to pay off his debts and to provide for Zelda's medical fees and the education of his daughter, Scottie. But there was another reason: writing was his life. He was too dedicated to give up. The result was his most complex and perhaps his greatest book, *Tender is the Night*, and another novel, *The Last Tycoon*, an unfinished work of real power based on his experiences as a Hollywood script-writer, as well as numerous short stories, some of which are among the best he wrote. He even discovered, in the Pat Hobby stories, that failure – his favourite theme – could be funny. His letters also testify that he had not given up at the end. He still went on the occasional bender, but now he was able 'to get sober enough to tolerate being sober'. There was in fact a new maturity about his attitude to life which makes him a far more interesting character than in the 1920s, now his 'lost decade'. There was less 'happiness and pleasure' than before, but there were what he called 'the deeper satisfactions that come out of struggle'. This was dear-bought wisdom indeed, of the type obtained by persisting in one's folly. At any rate the adolescent qualities, both good and bad, which he exhibited in the 1920s had been replaced by a new dignity. His talent, like his money, now needed to be husbanded in a way not to be conceived earlier, but it was still there, and so was the intense craftsmanship which had characterised all his work. He managed to add substantially to his oeuvre.

Interest in Scott Fitzgerald has always stemmed partly from his life story. He is often depicted as a gorgeous Icarus, a heroic figure whose descent was as rapid as his rise had been glorious, the victim of excessive early praise whose talent was tragically

Introduction

unfulfilled. All the world, it seems, loves this kind of ambiguous failure. There are indeed tragic aspects to his tumultuous life – as well as farcical and disreputable ones – and had he lived longer he might have surpassed his earlier achievements. But, in the end, it is his completed work that matters, and he wrote enough for success far to outweigh failure. Towards the end of his life he 'nursed the delusion' that there was 'some sort of epic grandeur' about his achievement. Most will decide that this was a fair description. To adapt Hemingway, life had destroyed him – almost – but had not defeated him.

Fitzgerald's writings are among the most readable and memorable in twentieth-century literature. There are rich elements of poetry in his books, and consequently he is to be read slowly and savoured. Those who rush ahead, pimping for the plot, will miss the best that he has to offer. It is the same with his sayings. Reflecting every phase and mood of his life, they are witty and down-to-earth, sparklingly superficial and dourly profound, gorgeously romantic and despairingly pessimistic. They bespeak a mind of lucid intelligence and reflect a deft and deathless artistry. Few authors who wrote so little can have left behind such rich seams. (Did anyone ever anatomise so acutely the pleasures and perils of alcohol or describe so well the romantic atmosphere of youthful expectations, the allure of money or the poignancy of regret?) He captured all the varied moods of his life, and we will all extract different gems.

R.D.P.

Quotations from Scott Fitzgerald's novels are given, in each section, in the order in which they were written. His short stories have been collected into several different sets of volumes, and therefore they are identified by the story's title only. Extracts from his letters are taken from Andrew Turnbull's edition (1964).

The United States of America

It is too soon to write about the Jazz Age [1919-29] with perspective, and without being suspected of premature arteriosclerosis ... Yet the present writer already looks back to it with nostalgia. It bore him up, flattered him and gave him more money than he had dreamed of, simply for telling people that he felt as they did, that something had to be done with all the nervous energy stored up and unexpended in the War.

'Echoes of the Jazz Age'

Though the Jazz Age continued, it became less and less an affair of youth. The sequel was like a children's party taken over by the elders, leaving the children puzzled and rather neglected and rather taken aback.

Ibid.

The word jazz in its progress towards respectability has meant first sex, then dancing, then music. It is associated with a state of nervous stimulation, not unlike that of big cities behind the lines of a war.

Ibid.

... the whole upper tenth of a nation living with the insouciance of grand dukes and the casualness of chorus girls.

Ibid.

New York had all the iridescence of the beginning of the world.

'My Lost City'

Effort per se had no dignity against the mere bounty of those days in New York ... a depreciatory word was found for it: a successful programme became a racket – I was in the literary racket.

Ibid.

As the toiler must live in the city's belly, so I was compelled to live in its disordered mind. *Ibid.*

The city was bloated, glutted, stupid with cakes and circuses, and a new expression 'Oh yeah?' summed up all the enthusiasm evoked by the announcement of the last super-skyscrapers. *Ibid.*

That most obnoxious type of countryman who lives near a metropolis and has attained its cheap smartness without its urbanity.

The Beautiful and Damned

Americans, while willing, even eager, to be serfs, have always been obstinate about being peasantry.

The Great Gatsby

I love New York on summer afternoons when everyone's away. There's something very sensuous about it – overripe, as if all sorts of funny fruits were going to fall into your hands. *Ibid.*

For a transitory enchanted moment man must have held his breath in the presence of this continent, compelled into an aesthetic contemplation he neither understood nor desired, face to face for the last time in history with something commensurate to his capacity for wonder.

Ibid.

There are no second acts in American lives.

The Last Tycoon

America's greatest promise is that something is going to happen, and after a while you get tired of waiting because nothing happens to people except that they grow old, and nothing happens to American art because America is the story of the moon that never rose.

The Letters, October 1925

America is so decadent that its brilliant children are damned almost before they are born.

Ibid.

Dreams

It isn't given to us to know those rare moments when people are wide open and the lightest touch can wither or heal. A moment too late and we can never reach them any more in this world. They will not be cured by our most efficacious drugs or slain with our sharpest words.

'Basil: The Freshest Boy'

A man who was aware that there could be no honour and yet had honour, who knew the sophistry of courage and yet was brave.

The Beautiful and Damned

Only the romanticist preserves the things worth preserving.

Ibid.

I always believe anything anyone tells me about myself – don't you?

Ibid.

One of those immortal moments which come so radiantly that their remembered light is enough to see by for years.

Ibid.

There's no beauty without poignancy and there's no poignancy without the feeling that it's going, men, names, books, houses – bound for dust – mortal –

Ibid.

Things are sweeter when they're lost.

Ibid.

Trying to preserve a century by keeping its relics up to date is like keeping a dying man alive by stimulants.

Ibid.

Desire just cheats you. It's like a sunbeam skipping here and there about a room. It stops and gilds some inconsequential object, and we poor fools try to grasp it – but when we do the sunbeam moves on to something else, and you've got the inconsequential part, but the glitter that made you want it is gone.

Ibid.

That illusion of young romantic love to which women look forever forward and forever back.

Ibid.

The fruit of youth or of the grape, the transitory magic of the brief passage from darkness to darkness – the old illusion that truth and beauty were in some way entwined.

Ibid.

I wanted no more riotous excursions with privileged glimpses into the human heart.

The Great Gatsby

If personality is an unbroken series of gestures, then there was something gorgeous about him, some heightened sensitivity to the promises of life, as if he were related to one of those intricate machines that register earthquakes ten thousand miles away.

Ibid.

I had that familiar conviction that life was beginning over again with the summer.

Ibid.

Tom would drift on forever seeking, a little wistfully, for the dramatic turbulence of some irrecoverable football game.

Ibid.

It was the kind of voice that the ear follows up and down, as if each speech is an arrangement of notes that will never be played again.

Ibid.

It was testimony to the romantic speculation he inspired that there were whispers about him from those who had found little it was necessary to whisper about in this world. *Ibid.*

It was one of those rare smiles with a quality of eternal reassurance in it, that you may come across four or five times in life. It faced – or seemed to face – the whole eternal world for an instant, and then concentrated on *you* with an irresistible prejudice in your favour. It understood you just so far as you wanted to be understood, believed in you as you would like to believe in yourself, and assured you that it had precisely the impression of you that, at your best, you hoped to convey. *Ibid.*

He came alive to me, delivered suddenly from the womb of his purposeless splendour.

Ibid.

He had been full of the idea so long, dreamed it right through to the end, waited with his teeth set, so to speak, at an inconceivable pitch of intensity. Now, in the reaction, he was running down like an over-wound clock. *Ibid.*

No amount of fire or freshness can challenge what a man can store up in his ghostly heart.

Ibid.

I think that voice held him most, with its fluctuating, feverish warmth, because it couldn't be over-dreamed – that voice was a deathless song.

Ibid.

His imagination had never really accepted them as his parents at all. The truth was that Jay Gatsby ... sprang from his Platonic conception of himself. He was a son of God – a phrase which, if it means anything, means just that – and he must be about His Father's business, the service of a vast, vulgar, and meretricious beauty.

Ibid.

The Sayings of F. Scott Fitzgerald

Reveries provided an outlet for his imagination; they were a satisfactory hint of the unreality of reality, a promise that the rock of the world was founded securely on a fairy's wing.

Ibid.

'Can't repeat the past?' he cried incredulously. 'Why of course you can!'

Ibid.

Gatsby saw that the blocks of the sidewalks really formed a ladder and mounted to a secret place above the trees – he could climb to it, if he climbed alone, and once there he could suck on the pap of life, gulp down the incomparable milk of wonder.

Ibid.

He knew that when he kissed this girl, and forever wed his unutterable vision to her perishable breath, his mind would never romp again like the mind of God.

Ibid.

… the green light, the orgastic future that year by year recedes before us. It eluded us then, but that's no matter – to-morrow we will run faster, stretch out our arms further … . And one fine morning –
So we beat on, boats against the current, borne back ceaselessly into the past.

Ibid.

There are always those to whom all self-revelation is contemptible, unless it ends with a noble thanks to the gods for the Unconquerable Soul.

The Crack-Up

Splendour is something in the heart.

Tender is the Night

He cherished the parvenu's passionate loyalty to an imaginary past.

The Last Tycoon

Intoxication

Their elders, tired of watching the carnival with ill-concealed envy, had discovered that young liquor would take the place of young blood.
'Echoes of the Jazz Age'

There were very few people left at the sober table. One of its former glories, the less sought-after girls who had become resigned to sublimating a probable celibacy, came across Freud and Jung in seeking their intellectual recompense and came tearing back into the fray.

Ibid.

The hangover became a part of the day as well allowed-for as the Spanish siesta.
'My Lost City'

Most of my friends drank too much – the more they were in tune with the times the more they drank.

Ibid.

How many weeks or months of dissipation to arrive at that condition of utter irresponsibility?
'Babylon Revisited'

He was a pretentious fool, making careers out of cocktails and meanwhile regretting, weakly and secretly, the collapse of an insufficient and wretched idealism.
The Beautiful and Damned

'You have something to drink every day and you're only twenty-five. Haven't you any ambition? Think what you'll be at forty.'
'I sincerely trust that I won't live that long.'

Ibid.

He was very drunk even then, so drunk as not to realize his own drunkenness. *Ibid.*

Wine gave a sort of gallantry to their own failure.

Ibid.

He doesn't show it any more unless he can hardly stand up, and he talks all right until he gets excited. He talks much better than he does when he's sober.

Ibid.

There was a kindliness about intoxication – there was that indescribable gloss and glamour it gave, like the memories of ephemeral and faded evenings.

Ibid.

All these people were too weary to be exhilarated by any ordinary stimulant; for weeks they had drunk cocktails before meals like Americans, wines and brandies like Frenchmen, beer like Germans, whisky-and-soda like the English, and as they were no longer in the twenties, this preposterous *mélange*, that was like some gigantic cocktail in a nightmare, served only to make them temporarily less conscious of the mistakes of the night before.

'The Bridal Party'

People disappeared, reappeared, made plans to go somewhere, and then lost each other, searched for each other, found each other a few feet away.

The Great Gatsby

In his blue gardens men and girls came and went like moths among the whisperings and the champagne and the stars.

Ibid.

I slunk off in the direction of the cocktail table – the only place in the garden where a single man could linger without looking purposeless and alone.

Ibid.

I was on my way to get roaring drunk from sheer embarrassment.

Ibid.

I've been drunk for about a week now, and I thought it might sober me up to sit in a library.

Ibid.

I had taken two finger-bowls of champagne, and the scene had changed before my eyes into something significant, elemental, and profound.

Ibid.

I like large parties. They're so intimate. At small parties there isn't any privacy.

Ibid.

It's a great advantage not to drink among hard-drinking people. You can hold your tongue and, moreover, you can time any little irregularity of your own so that everybody else is so blind that they don't see or care.

Ibid.

They were both in the gray gentle world of a mild hangover of fatigue when the nerves relax in bunches like piano strings, and crackle suddenly like wicker chairs.

Tender is the Night

Tell a secret over the radio, publish it in a tabloid, but never tell it to a man who drinks more than three or four a day.

Ibid.

Trouble is when you're sober you don't want to see anybody, and when you're tight nobody wants to see you.

Ibid.

The drink made past happy things contemporary with the present, as if they were still going on, contemporary even with the future as if they were about to happen again.

Ibid.

The Sayings of F. Scott Fitzgerald

Often people display a curious respect for a man drunk, rather like the respect of simple races for the insane. Respect rather than fear. There is something awe-inspiring in one who has lost all inhibitions, who will do anything.

Ibid.

There are those who can drink and those who can't. Obviously Dick can't. You ought to tell him not to.

Ibid.

Certain classes of English people lived upon a concentrated essence of the anti-social that, in comparison, reduced the gorgings of New York to something like a child contracting indigestion from ice cream.

Ibid.

When he buys his ties he has to ask if gin will make them run.

The Crack-Up

He was so transparent that you could almost watch the alcohol mingle with the poison of his exhaustion.

The Last Tycoon

First you take a drink, then the drink takes a drink, then the drink takes you.

Attributed

Youth, Age & Education

It is youth's felicity as well as its insufficiency that it can never live in the present, but must always be measuring up the day against its own radiantly imagined future – flowers and gold, girls and stars, they are only pre-figurations and prophecies of that incomparable, unattainable young dream.

'The Diamond as Big as the Ritz'

Everybody's youth is a dream, a form of chemical madness.

Ibid.

The second half of life is a long process of getting rid of things.

'Three Hours Between Planes'

… the flustered cynicism which is the fate of all headmasters and settles on them like green mould.

'Basil: The Freshest Boy'

After the sureties of youth there sets in a period of intense and intolerable complexity.

The Beautiful and Damned

It is a simple soul indeed to whom as many things are significant and meaningful at thirty as at ten years before.

Ibid.

You're not learning anything – you're just getting tired.

Ibid.

Something was making him nibble at the edge of stale ideas as if his sturdy physical egotism no longer nourished his peremptory heart.

The Great Gatsby

He's so dumb he doesn't know he's alive.

Ibid.

... a persistent undergraduate given to violent innuendo, and obviously under the impression that sooner or later Jordan was going to yield him up her person to a greater or lesser degree.

Ibid.

He went to Oggsford College in England. You know Oggsford College? ... It's one of the most famous colleges in the world.

Ibid.

He had reached an age where death no longer has the quality of ghastly surprise.

Ibid.

'I'm thirty,' I said. 'I'm five years too old to lie to myself and call it honour.'

Ibid.

For some months he had been going through that partitioning of the things of youth wherein it is decided whether or not to die for what one no longer believes.

Tender is the Night

Eighteen might look at thirty-four through a rising mist of adolescence; but twenty-two would see thirty-eight with discerning clarity.

Ibid.

... the fine quiet of the scholar which is nearest of all things to heavenly peace.

Ibid.

The more you know, the more there is just beyond, and it keeps on coming.

The Last Tycoon

Whole months go by and nothing seems to happen. Is that just middle-age?

The Letters, April 1937

I knew in my heart that I had missed something by being a poor Latin scholar, like a blessed evening with a lovely girl. It was a great human experience I had rejected through laziness, through having sown no painful seed.

Ibid., February 1938

Life promises so very much to a pretty girl between the ages of sixteen and twenty-five that she never quite recovers from it.

Ibid., 16 March 1938

None of our colleges have succeeded in inventing anything to compete with the kind of love that doesn't have to be paid for with responsibility.

Ibid.

If you will trust my scheme of making a mental habit of doing the hard thing first, when you are absolutely fresh, and I mean doing the *hardest* thing *first* at the *exact moment that you feel yourself fit for doing anything* in any particular period, morning, afternoon or evening, you will go a long way toward mastering the principle of concentration.

Ibid., 18 April 1938

The young can't believe in the youth of their fathers.

Ibid., 7 July 1938

The adolescent offers nothing, can do nothing, say nothing that the adult cannot do better.

Ibid.

Who is interested in a girl with her bloom worn off at sixteen?

Ibid., 19 November 1938

A great social success is a pretty girl who plays her cards as carefully as if she were plain.

Ibid.

Remember – there's an awful disease that overtakes popular girls at 19 or 20 called emotional bankruptcy.
Ibid., 25 January 1940

That is one way to grow learned, first pretend to be – then have to live up to it.
Ibid., 6 July 1940

Is your generation so soft that they talk of going to pieces if life doesn't always present itself in terms of beautiful, easy decisions?
Ibid., 24 August 1940

Success & Failure

One gradually developed a protective hardness against both praise and blame. Too often people liked your things for the wrong reasons or people liked them whose dislike would be a compliment.

'Early Success'

Premature success gives one an almost mystical conception of destiny as opposed to will-power – at its worst the Napoleonic delusion. The man who arrives young believes that he exercises his will because his star is shining. The man who only asserts himself at thirty has a balanced idea of what will-power and fate have each contributed, the one who gets there at forty is liable to put the emphasis on will alone.

Ibid.

He believed in character ... as the eternally valuable element. Everything else wore out.

'Babylon Revisited'

He suddenly realized the meaning of the word 'dissipate' – to dissipate into thin air; to make nothing out of something.

Ibid.

He had, indeed, become the scapegoat, the immediate villain, the sponge which absorbed all malice and irritability abroad – just as the most frightened person in a party seems to absorb all the others' fear, seemed to be afraid for them all.

'Basil: The Freshest Boy'

He had gathered that life for everybody was a struggle, sometimes magnificent from a distance, but always difficult and surprisingly simple and a little sad.

Ibid.

One takes what one can, up to the limit of one's strength.
'The Bridal Party'

What I want to know is, what happens to people like me who aren't able to forget?

Ibid.

Boredom, which is another name and a frequent disguise for vitality.

The Beautiful and Damned

Intelligence is little more than a short foot-rule by which we measure the infinite achievements of Circumstances.

Ibid.

They themselves were not confused, because there was nothing in them to be confused – they changed phrases from month to month as they changed neckties.

Ibid.

The successful man tells his son to profit by his father's good fortune, and the failure tells *his* son to profit by his father's mistakes.

Ibid.

Almost any exhibition of complete self-sufficiency draws a stunned tribute from me.

The Great Gatsby

To a certain temperament the situation might have seemed intriguing – my own instinct was to telephone immediately for the police.

Ibid.

Everyone suspects himself of at least one of the cardinal virtues, and this is mine: I am one of the few honest people that I have ever known.

Ibid.

There are only the pursued, the pursuing, the busy, and the tired.

Ibid.

There was no difference between men, in intelligence or race, so profound as the difference between the sick and the well.

Ibid.

There is no confusion like the confusion of a simple mind.

Ibid.

I wanted to leave things in order and not just trust that obliging and indifferent sea to sweep my refuse away.

Ibid.

... the too obtrusive fate that herded its inhabitants along a short-cut from nothing to nothing.

Ibid.

Of course all life is a process of breaking down, but the blows that do the dramatic side of the work – the big sudden blows that come, or seem to come, from outside – the ones you remember and blame things on and, in moments of weakness, tell your friends about, don't show their effect all at once. There is another sort of blow that comes from within – that you don't feel until it's too late to do anything about it, until you realize with finality that in some regard you will never be as good a man again. The first sort of breakage seems to happen quick – the second kind happens almost without your knowing it but is realized suddenly indeed.

The Crack-Up

Life was something you dominated if you were any good. Life yielded easily to intelligence and effort, or to what proportion could be mustered of both.

Ibid.

The ego would continue as an arrow shot from nothingness to nothingness with such force that only gravity would bring it to earth at last.

Ibid.

Of all natural forces, vitality is the incommunicable one.

Ibid.

Vitality never 'takes'. You have it or you haven't it, like health or brown eyes or honour or a baritone voice.

Ibid.

A man does not recover from such jolts – he becomes a different person and, eventually, the new person finds new things to care about.

Ibid.

A clean break is something you cannot come back from; that is irretrievable because it makes the past cease to exist.

Ibid.

Remember that when you are struggling and fighting and perhaps feeling you are getting nowhere, maybe even despairing – those are the times when you may be making slow, sure progress.

The Letters, December 1938

Money

Let me tell you about the very rich. They are different
from you and me. They possess and enjoy early, and it
does something to them, makes them soft where we are
hard, and cynical where we are trustful.

'The Rich Boy'

Money and power were falling into the hands of people
in comparison with whom the leader of a village Soviet
would be a gold-mine of judgement and culture.

'Echoes of the Jazz Age'

The idea that to make a man work you've got to hold
gold in front of his eyes is a growth, not an axiom. We've
done that for so long that we've forgotten there's any
other way.

This Side of Paradise

It is essentially cleaner to be corrupt and rich than it is to
be innocent and poor.

Ibid.

An aristocracy founded sheerly on money postulates
wealth in the particular.

The Beautiful and Damned

Everybody I knew was in the bond business, so I
supposed it could support one more single man.

The Great Gatsby

They had spent a year in France for no particular reason,
and then drifted here and there unrestfully wherever
people played polo and were rich together.

Ibid.

Her voice is full of money.

Ibid.

Gatsby was overwhelmingly aware of the youth and mystery that wealth imprisons and preserves, of the freshness of many clothes, and of Daisy, gleaming like silver, safe and proud above the hot struggles of the poor.

Ibid.

They were careless people, Tom and Daisy – they smashed up things and creatures and then retreated back into their money or their vast carelessness, or whatever it was that kept them together, and let other people clean up the mess they had made.

Ibid.

We're a rich person's clinic – we don't use the word nonsense.

Tender is the Night

… an abiding distrust, an animosity, towards the leisure class – not the conviction of a revolutionist but the smouldering hatred of a peasant.

The Crack-Up

All big men spend money freely. I hate avarice or even caution.

The Letters, June 1930

Business is a dull game and they pay a big price in human values for their money.

Ibid., 24 August 1940

Advertising is a racket, like the movies and the brokerage business. You cannot be honest without admitting that its constructive contribution to humanity is exactly minus zero. It is simply a means of making dubious promises to a credulous public.

Ibid.

Sex & the Sexes

There are all kinds of love in the world, but never the same love twice.

'The Sensible Thing'

I remember a perfectly mated, contented young mother asking my wife's advice about 'having an affair right away', though she had no one especially in mind, 'because don't you think it's sort of undignified when you get much over thirty?'

'Echoes of the Jazz Age'

As Ernest Hemingway once remarked, the sole purpose of the cabaret is for unattached men to find complaisant women. All the rest is a wasting of time in bad air.

'My Lost City'

The shows were broader, the buildings were higher, the morals were looser and the liquor was cheaper; but all these benefits did not really minister to much delight. Young people wore out early – they were hard and languid at twenty-one.

Ibid.

She was a faded but still lovely woman of twenty-seven.

'Early Success'

They had been married three years, and they were much more in love than that implies. It was seldom that they hated each other with that violent hate of which only young couples are capable.

'Gretchen's Forty Winks'

She was still so physically appealing that you wanted to touch the personality that trembled on her lips.

'The Last of the Belles'

There remained to her only a persistent, a physical hope; hope in her stomach that there was someone whom she would love more than he loved her.

'Josephine: A Woman with a Past'

Josephine, who had always believed that boys and girls were made for nothing but each other, and as soon as possible.

Ibid.

Save in the very young, only love begets love.

Ibid.

One mustn't run through people, and, for the sake of a romantic half-hour, trade a possibility that might develop – quite seriously – later, at the proper time. She did not know that this was the first mature thought that she had ever made in her life, but it was.

Ibid.

Her voice was flip as a whip and cold as automatic refrigeration, in the mode grown familiar since British ladies took to piecing themselves together out of literature.

'Two Wrongs'

She could feel him slipping out of her heart, feel the space he left, and all at once he was gone, and she could even forgive him and be sorry for him. All this in a minute.

Ibid.

To her, dancing meant that elaborate blend of tortuous attitudes and formal pirouettes that evolved out of Italy several hundred years ago and reached its apogee in Russia at the beginning of this century.

Ibid.

What happened just now? When we just pour towards each other like we used to – as if we were one person, as if the same blood was flowing through both of us?

'The Bridal Party'

It seems to me that the average man nowadays just asks to be made a monkey of by some woman who doesn't even get any fun out of reducing him to that level.

Ibid.

Sorrow's a lot of fun for most women and for some men, but it seems to me that a marriage ought to be based on hope.

Ibid.

After a pretty woman has had her first child, she's very vulnerable, because she wants to be reassured about her own charm. She's got to have some new man's unqualified devotion to prove to herself she hasn't lost anything.

'Crazy Sunday'

The psychoanalyst told Miles that he had a mother complex. In his first marriage he transferred his mother complex to his wife, you see – and then his sex turned to me. But when we married the thing repeated itself – he transferred his mother complex to me and all his libido turned towards this other woman.

Ibid.

She hovered somewhere between the realest of realities and the most blatant of impersonations.

Ibid.

She had once been a Catholic, but discovering that priests are infinitely more attentive when she was in process of losing or regaining faith in Mother Church, she maintained an enchantingly wavering attitude.

This Side of Paradise

A big man has no time really to do anything but just sit and be big.

Ibid.

Gloria's darn nice – not a brain in her head.

The Beautiful and Damned

What he means by brains in a woman ... is a smattering of literary misinformation.

Ibid.

We're growing old, Anthony. I'm twenty-seven, by God! Three years to thirty, and then I'm what an undergraduate calls a middle-aged man.

Ibid.

A gentleman ... A man who prefers the first edition of a book to the last edition of a newspaper.

Ibid.

It was agony to comprehend her beauty in a glance.

Ibid.

What grubworms women are to crawl on their bellies through colourless marriages!

Ibid.

The night-clerk at the Hotel Lacfadio refused to admit them, on the grounds that they were not married. The clerk thought that Gloria was beautiful. He did not think that anything so beautiful as Gloria could be moral.

Ibid.

He had had one of those sudden flashes of illumination vouchsafed to all men who are dominated by a strong and beloved woman, which shows them a world of harder men, more fiercely trained and grappling with the abstractions of thought and war.

Ibid.

'Women soil easily,' she said, 'far more easily than men.'

Ibid.

He was capable of short attractions towards other women, the hitherto-suppressed outcroppings of an experimental temperament.

Ibid.

Women like dark imperfect jewels, women like vegetables, women like great bags of abominably dirty laundry.

Ibid.

Muriel doesn't mean to tell everyone she knows ... but she thinks everyone she tells is the only one she's going to tell.

Ibid.

After that reflowering of tenderness and passion each of them had returned into some solitary dream unshared by the other and what endearments passed between them passed, it seemed, from empty heart to empty heart, echoing hollowly the departure of what they knew at last had gone.

Ibid.

He was the sort who dined with two girls rather than with one – his imagination was almost incapable of sustaining a dialogue.

Ibid.

The intimate revelations of young men, or at least the terms in which they express them, are usually plagiaristic and marred by obvious suppressions.

The Great Gatsby

One of those men who reach such an acute limited excellence at twenty-one that everything afterward savours of anti-climax.

Ibid.

'Now, don't think my opinion on these matters is final,' he seemed to say, 'just because I'm stronger and more of a man than you are.'

Ibid.

I've heard it said that Daisy's murmur was only to make people lean toward her; an irrelevant criticism that made it no less charming.

Ibid.

That's the best thing a girl can be in this world, a beautiful little fool.

Ibid.

I think I'll arrange a marriage. Come over often, Nick, and I'll sort of – oh – fling you together. You know – lock you up accidentally in linen closets and push you out to sea in a boat, and all that sort of thing –

Ibid.

With the influence of her dress her personality had also undergone a change. The intense vitality that had been so remarkable ... was converted into impressive *hauteur*.

Ibid.

I was so excited that when I got into a taxi with him I didn't hardly know I wasn't getting into a subway train. All I kept thinking about, over and over, was 'You can't live forever; you can't live forever.'

Ibid.

I wasn't actually in love, but I felt a sort of tender curiosity.

Ibid.

He knew women early, and since they spoiled him he became contemptuous of them, of young virgins because they were ignorant, of the others because they were hysterical about things which in his overwhelming self-absorption he took for granted.

Ibid.

If you want to kiss me any time during the evening, Nick, just let me know and I'll arrange it for you. Just mention my name. Or present a green card. I'm giving out green –

Ibid.

That anyone should care in this heat whose flushed lips he kissed, whose head made damp the pyjama pocket over his heart!

Ibid.

He was his wife's man and not his own.

Ibid.

He took what he could get, ravenously and unscrupulously – eventually he took Daisy one still October night, took her because he had no real right to touch her hand.

Ibid.

He knew that Daisy was extraordinary, but he didn't realize just how extraordinary a 'nice' girl could be ... He felt married to her, that was all.

Ibid.

What was the use of doing great things if I could have a better time telling her what I was going to do?

Ibid.

She wanted her life shaped now, immediately – and the decision must be made by some force – of love, of money, of unquestionable practicality – that was close at hand.

Ibid.

I'm vain as a woman. If anybody pretends to be interested in me, I'll ask for more.

Ibid.

She was lovelier now at twenty-four than she had been at eighteen, when her hair was brighter than she.

Tender is the Night

He sometimes looked back with awe at the carnivals of affection he had given as a general might gaze upon a massacre he had ordered to satisfy an impersonal blood lust.

Ibid.

... the wife of an arriviste who had not arrived.

Ibid.

Well, you never knew exactly how much space you occupied in people's lives.

Ibid.

A man can't live without a moral code. Mine is that I'm against the burning of witches. Whenever they burn a witch I get all hot under the collar.

Ibid.

They would all three have made alternatively good courtesans or good wives not by the accident of birth but through the greater accident of finding their man or not finding him.

Ibid.

Her love had reached a point where now at last she was beginning to be unhappy.

Ibid.

Like most women she liked to be told how she should feel.

Ibid.

Often a man can play the helpless child in front of a woman, but he can almost never bring it off when he feels most like a helpless child.

Ibid.

… her body calculated to a millimetre to suggest a bud yet guarantee a flower.

Ibid.

She smiled, a moving childish smile that was like all the lost youth in the world.

Ibid.

Women are necessarily capable of almost anything in their struggle for survival and can scarcely be convicted of such man-made crimes as 'cruelty'.

Ibid.

Sex & the Sexes

It would be hundreds of years before any emergent Amazons would ever grasp the fact that a man is vulnerable only in his pride, but delicate as Humpty Dumpty once that is meddled with.

Ibid.

'You know, you're a little complicated after all.'
'Oh no,' she assured him hastily. 'No, I'm not really – I'm just a – I'm just a whole lot of different simple people.'

Ibid.

Without being an old maid, she was, like most self-made women, rather old maidish.

The Last Tycoon

I like people and I like them to like me, but I wear my heart where God put it – on the inside.

Ibid.

Emotionally, at least, people can't live by taking in each other's washing.

Ibid.

When a girl tells the man she likes second best about the other one – then she's in love.

Ibid.

She was twenty-five or so. It would have been a waste if she had not loved and been loved.

Ibid.

'Are you surprised?'
'At what?'
'That we're two people again. Don't you always think – hope that you'll be one person, and then find you're still two?'

Ibid.

I don't know now exactly the colour of your eyes, but they make me sorry for everyone in the world.

Ibid.

He was as attractive as men can be who don't really care about women as such.

Ibid.

Like many men, he did not like flowers except a few weedy ones – they were too highly evolved and self-conscious. But he liked leaves and peeled twigs, horse chestnuts and even acorns, unripe, ripe and wormy fruit.

Ibid.

It's fun to stretch and see the blue heavens spreading once more, spreading azure thighs for adventure.

Ibid.

I think if a suitor of Scottie's was entirely innocent in his past life I'd be inclined to make the old remark: 'Well, I don't want you to practise on her.'

The Letters, 21 September 1932

A girl having lost a man is liable to suddenly build him up into the only man in the world when, had things run smoothly, it is doubtful if he would have long interested her.

Ibid., 20 July 1939

The faces of most American women over thirty are relief maps of petulant and bewildered unhappiness.

Ibid., 5 October 1940

When a man is tired of life at 21 it indicates that he is rather tired of something in himself.

Ibid., 29 November 1940

Lois Moran used to worry because all the attractive men she knew were married. She finally inverted it into the credo that if a man *wasn't* married and inaccessible, he wasn't a first-rate man. She gave herself a very bad time.

Ibid.

Hollywood

We don't work too hard in Hollywood ... Everything is 'Manana' – in Spanish that means tomorrow.
'Fun in an Artist's Studio'

Those few who decide things are happy in their work and sure that they are worthy of their hire – the rest live in a mist of doubt as to when their vast inadequacy will be disclosed.
'Pat Hobby and Orson Welles'

He was the perennial man of promise in American letters – what he could actually do with words was astounding, they glowed and coruscated – he wrote sentences, paragraphs, chapters that were masterpieces of fine weaving and spinning. It was only when I met some poor devil of a screen writer who had been trying to make a logical story out of one of his books that I realized he had his enemies.
'Financing Finnegan'

Gary Cooper came in and sat down in a corner with a bunch of men who breathed whenever he did and looked as if they lived off him and weren't budging.
The Last Tycoon

This is a tragic city of beautiful girls – the girls who mop the floor are beautiful, the waitresses, the shop ladies. You never want to see any more beauty.
The Letters, Winter 1927

She [Joan Crawford] can't change her emotions in the middle of a scene without going through a sort of Jekyll and Hyde contortion of the face, so that when one wants to indicate that she is going from joy to sorrow, one must cut away and then cut back. Also, you can never give her such a stage direction as 'telling a lie', because if you did, she would practically give a representation of Benedict Arnold selling West Point to the British.
Ibid., 11 March 1938

Somehow conditions in the industry propose the paradox: 'We brought you here for your individuality but while you're here we insist that you do everything to conceal it.'

Ibid., 25 February 1939

... one of those brilliant Hollywood reputations which endure all of two months sometimes.

Ibid., 11 May 1940

Himself

I began to bawl because I had everything I wanted and knew I would never be so happy again.

'My Lost City'

I had been only a mediocre caretaker of most of the things left in my own hands, even of my talent.

The Crack-Up

In a single morning I would go through the emotions ascribable to Wellington at Waterloo. I lived in a world of inscrutable hostiles and inalienable friends and supporters.   *Ibid.*

After about an hour of solitary pillow-hugging, I began to realize that for two years my life had been a drawing on resources that I did not possess, but I had been mortgaging myself physically and spiritually up to the hilt.   *Ibid.*

Hating the night when I couldn't sleep and hating the day because it went towards night.

Ibid.

A feeling that I was standing at twilight on a deserted range, with an empty rifle in my hands and the targets down. No problem set – simply a silence with only the sound of my own breathing.   *Ibid.*

I was forced into a measure that no one adopts voluntarily: I was impelled to think. God, was it difficult!

Ibid.

It was strange to have no self – to be like a little boy left alone in a big house, who knew that now he could do anything he wanted to do, but found that there was nothing that he wanted to do.

Ibid.

I only wanted absolute quiet to think out why I had developed a sad attitude towards sadness, a melancholy attitude towards melancholy, and a tragic attitude towards tragedy – *why I had become identified with the objects of my horror or compassion.*

Ibid.

I must continue to be a writer because that was my only way of life, but I would cease any attempts to be a person – to be kind, just, or generous.

Ibid.

The old dream of being an entire man in the Goethe-Byron-Shaw tradition, with an opulent American touch ... has been relegated to the junk heap of the shoulder pads worn for one day on the Princeton freshman football field and the overseas cap never worn overseas.

Ibid.

This is what I think now: that the natural state of the sentient adult is a qualified unhappiness. I think also that in an adult the desire to be finer in grain than you are, 'a constant striving' (as those people say who gain their bread by saying it) only adds to this unhappiness in the end – that end that comes to our youth and hope.

Ibid.

My own happiness in the past often approached such an ecstasy that I could not share it even with the person dearest to me but had to walk it away in quiet streets and lanes with only fragments of it to distil into little lines in books – and I think that my happiness, or talent or self-delusion or what you will, was an exception. It was not the natural thing but the unnatural – unnatural as the Boom; and my recent experience parallels the wave of despair that swept the nation when the Boom was over.

Ibid.

I will try to be a correct animal ... and if you throw me a bone with enough meat on it I may even lick your hand.

Ibid.

Himself [47]

I talk with the authority of failure – Ernest [Hemingway] with the authority of success.

Ibid.

For a shy man it was nice to be somebody except oneself again: to be 'the Author' as one had been 'the Lieutenant'. Of course one wasn't really an author any more than one had been an army officer, but nobody seemed to guess behind the false face.

'Early Success'

I'm sick of the flabby semi-intellectual softness in which I flounder with my generation.

The Letters, 25 August 1921

I cannot let it go out unless it has the very best I'm capable of in it, or even, as I feel sometimes, something better than I'm capable of.

Ibid., 16 April 1924

I don't know anyone who has used up so much personal experience as I have at 27. *Ibid.*

I think my novel [*The Great Gatsby*] is about the best American novel ever.

Ibid., 27 August 1924

You remember I used to say I wanted to die at thirty – well, I'm now twenty-nine and the prospect is still welcome. My work is the only thing that makes me happy – except to be a little tight – and for those two indulgences I pay a big price in mental and physical hangovers. *Ibid.*, December 1925

The more I get for my trash, the less I can bring myself to write. *Ibid.*, December 1925

Why shouldn't I go crazy? My father is a moron and my mother is a neurotic, half insane with pathological nervous worry. Between them they haven't and never have had the brains of Calvin Coolidge.

Ibid., 20 February 1926

So much has happened to me lately that I despair of ever assimilating it – or forgetting it, which is the same thing.
Ibid., 18 April 1927

To me the conditions of an artistically creative life are so arduous that I can only compare them to the duties of a soldier in war-time.
Ibid., Spring 1933

I never believe much in happiness. I never believe in misery either. Those are things you see on the stage or the screen or the printed page, they never really happen to you in life.
Ibid., 8 August 1933

I would rather be an artist than a careerist.
Ibid., 23 April 1934

Having once found the intensity of art, nothing else that can happen in life can ever again seem as important as the creative process.
Ibid.

I have honestly never gone in for hating.
Ibid., 1 June 1934

Outside interests generally mean for me women, liquor or some form of exhibitionism.
Ibid., 7 September 1934

I have drunk too much and that is certainly slowing me up. On the other hand, without drink I do not know whether I could have survived this long.
Ibid., 8 November 1934

I am feeling somewhat plucked and old as I approach forty.
Ibid., 24 April 1935

I didn't know till 15 that there was anyone in the world except me, and it cost me *plenty*.
Ibid., Summer, 1935

Common sense tells me that there are rules but, like all modern men, the shade of Rousseau haunts me.

Ibid., Fall, 1935

I can't give you the particular view of life that I have (which as you know is a tragic one), without dulling your enthusiasm. A whole lot of people have found life a whole lot of fun. I have not found it so. But I had a hell of a lot of fun when I was in my twenties and thirties; and I feel that it is your duty to accept the sadness, the tragedy of the world we live in, with a certain *esprit*.

Ibid., 17 November 1936

Am I the only best seller who doesn't sell?

Ibid., February 1937

I used to think that my sensory impression of the world came from outside. I used to actually believe that it was as objective as blue skies or a piece of music. Now I know it was within, and emphatically cherish what little is left.

Ibid., 11 March 1938

My generation of radicals and breakers-down never found anything to take the place of the old virtues of work and courage and the old graces of courtesy and politeness.

Ibid., July 1938

In one way you are like me – that when things seemed to be going oh so smoothly they were really slipping from underneath subtly and surely.

Ibid., December 1938

I would either be a miracle man or a hack if I could go on turning out an identical product for three decades.

Ibid., c. July 1939

Life has humbled me.

Ibid., Winter 1939

It's just that we feel so damned secure at times as long as there's enough in the bank to buy the next meal, and enough moral stuff in reserve to take us through the next ordeal. Our danger is imagining that we have resources – material and moral – which we haven't got.

Ibid., 5 April 1939

I am not a great man, but sometimes I think the impersonal and objective quality of my talent and the sacrifices of it, in pieces, to preserve its essential value has come sort of epic grandeur. Anyhow after hours I nurse myself with delusions of that sort.

Ibid., 31 October 1939

I guess I am too much a moralist at heart and really want to preach at people in some acceptable form rather than to entertain them.

Ibid., 4 November 1939

My God, what a fund of hope and belief I must have had in the old days!

Ibid., 31 January 1940

I can *understand* the overconfidence – God haven't I had it? But it's hard as hell to recognize it in oneself – especially when time's so short and there's so *much* we want to do.

Ibid., 27 March 1940

What little I've accomplished has been by the most laborious and uphill work, and I wish now I'd never relaxed or looked back – but said at the end of *The Great Gatsby*: 'I've found my line – from now on this comes first. This is my immediate duty – without which I am nothing.'

Ibid., 12 June 1940

The talent that matures early is usually of the poetic [type], which mine was in large part.

Ibid., 18 July 1940

Once one is caught up into the material world not one person in ten thousand finds the time to form literary taste, to examine the validity of philosophic concepts for himself, or to form what, for lack of a better phrase, I might call the wise and tragic sense of life. By this I mean the thing that lies behind all great careers, from Shakespeare's to Abraham Lincoln's, and as far back as there are books to read – the sense that life is essentially a cheat and its conditions are those of defeat, and that the redeeming things are not 'happiness and pleasure' but the deeper satisfactions that come out of struggle. Having learned this in theory from the lives and conclusions of great men, you can get a hell of a lot more enjoyment out of whatever bright things come your way.

Ibid., 5 October 1940

You have got two beautiful bad examples for parents. Just do everything we didn't do and you will be perfectly safe.

Ibid., December 1940

Literature & Writers

Begin with an individual, and before you know it you find that you have created a type; begin with a type, and you find that you have created – nothing.

'The Rich Boy'

A writer can spin on about his adventures after thirty, after forty, after fifty, but the criteria by which these adventures are weighed and valued are irrevocably settled at the age of twenty-five.

'Ring'

His career had started brilliantly, and if it had not kept up to its first exalted level, at least it started brilliantly all over again every few years.

'Financing Finnegan'

The notion of sitting down and conjuring up, not only words in which to clothe thoughts but thoughts worthy of being clothed – the whole thing was absurdly beyond his desires.

The Beautiful and Damned

You might know too much for your pen.   *Ibid.*

A classic ... is a successful book that has survived the reaction of the next period or generation. Then it's safe, like a style in architecture or furniture. It's acquired a picturesque dignity to take the place of its fashion.

Ibid.

It seemed a romantic business to be a successful literary man – you were never going to be as famous as a movie star but what note you had was probably longer-lived – you were never going to have the power of a man of strong political or religious convictions but you were certainly more independent. Of course within the practice of your trade you were forever unsatisfied – but I, for one, would not have chosen any other.

The Crack-Up

The novel ... was the strongest and supplest medium for conveying thought and emotion from one human being to another.

Ibid.

There never was a good biography of a good novelist. There couldn't be. He is too many people, if he's any good.

Ibid.

Mostly, we authors must repeat ourselves – that's the truth. We have two or three great moving experiences in our lives – experiences so great and moving that it doesn't seem at the time that anyone else has been caught up and pounded and dazzled and astonished and beaten and broken and rescued and illuminated and rewarded and humbled in just that way ever before.

Ibid.

Soon you will be writing little books called 'Deep Thoughts for the Layman', so simplified that they are positively guaranteed not to cause thinking.

Tender is the Night

Writers aren't people exactly. Or, if they're any good, they're a whole *lot* of people trying so hard to be one person.

The Last Tycoon

What people are ashamed of usually makes a good story.

Ibid.

I grew up thinking that writer and secretary were the same, except that a writer usually smelled of cocktails.

Ibid.

ACTION IS CHARACTER.

Ibid.

To write it, it took three months; to conceive it – three minutes; to collect the data on it – all my life.

The Letters, April 1920

An author ought to write for the youth of his own generation, the critics of the next, and the schoolmasters of ever afterward.

Ibid.

The one duty of a sincere writer – to set down life as he sees it as gracefully as he knows how.

Ibid., 28 December 1920

This is to tell you about a young man named Ernest Hemingway ... He's the real thing.

Ibid., 18 October 1924

Did you ever know a writer to calmly take a just criticism and shut up?

Ibid., 4 May 1925

People don't seem to realize that for an intelligent man writing down is about the hardest thing in the world.

Ibid.

I'm afraid I haven't quite reached the ruthless artistry which would let me cut out an exquisite bit that had no place in the context.

Ibid., 9 August 1925

... Ernest's [Hemingway's] quality of a stick hardened in the fire.

Ibid., 1 September 1930

You haven't been in the publishing business over twenty years without noticing the streaks of smallness in very large personalities.

Ibid., 14 May 1932

I have lived so long within the circle of this book [*Tender is the Night*] and with these characters that often it seems to me that the real world does not exist but that only these characters exist.

Ibid., 4 March 1934

The professional reviewers: the light men who bubble at the mouth with enthusiasm because they see other bubbles floating around, the dumb men who regularly mistake your worst stuff for your best and your best for your worst, and, most of all, the cowards who straddle and the leeches who review your books in terms that they have cribbed out of the book itself, like scholars under some extraordinary dispensation which allows them to heckle the teacher.
Ibid., 10 May 1934

You [Gertrude Stein] were the same fine fire to everyone who sat upon your hearth – for it was your hearth, because you carry home with you wherever you are – a home before which we have all always warmed ourselves.
Ibid., 29 December 1934

He [Thomas Wolfe] who has such infinite power of suggestion and delicacy has absolutely no right to glut people on whole meals of caviar.
Ibid., 17 April 1935

It is my contention that tiredness, boredom, exhaustion, etc., must not be conveyed by the symbols which they show in life, in fact, can't be so conveyed in literature because boredom is essentially boring and tiredness is essentially tiring.
Ibid.

Almost everything I write in novels goes, for better or worse, into the subconscious of the reader.
Ibid., August 1935

God, what a hell of a profession to be a writer. One is one simply because one can't help it.
Ibid.

Nobody ever became a writer just by wanting to be one. If you have anything to say, anything you feel nobody has ever said before, you have got to feel so desperately that you will find some way to say it that nobody has ever found before, so that the thing you have to say and the way of saying it blend as one matter – as indissolubly as if they were conceived together.
Ibid., 20 October 1936

Don't try to be witty in the writing, unless it's natural – just true and real. *Ibid.*, 7 July 1938

After reading Thoreau I felt how much I have lost by leaving nature out of my life.

Ibid., 11 March 1939

The strongest should come first in comedy because once a character is really established as funny everything he does becomes funny. At least it's that way in life.

Ibid., 9 March 1940

Often I think writing is a sheer paring away of oneself leaving always something thinner, barer, more meager.

Ibid., 27 April 1940

In the opinion of any real artist the inventor, which is to say Giotto or Leonardo, is infinitely superior to the finished Tintoretto, and the original D.H. Lawrence is infinitely greater than the Steinbecks.

Ibid., 7 May 1940

High-priced commercial writing for the magazines is a very definite trick.

Ibid., 19 May 1940

A good style simply doesn't form unless you absorb half a dozen top-flight authors every year. Or rather it *forms* but, instead of being a subconscious amalgam of all that you have admired, it is simply a reflection of the last writer you have read, a watered-down journalese.

Ibid., 18 July 1940

Poetry ... is the most concentrated form of style.

Ibid., 29 July 1940

Poetry is either something that lives like fire inside you – like music to the musician or Marxism to the Communist – or else it is nothing, an empty, formalized bore around which pedants can endlessly drone their notes and explanations.

Ibid., 3 August 1940

Literature & Writers

'The Grecian Urn' is unbearably beautiful with every syllable as inevitable as the notes in Beethoven's Ninth Symphony or it's just something you don't understand. It is what it is because an extraordinary genius paused at that point in history and touched it. I suppose I've read it a hundred times. About the tenth time I began to know what it was about, and caught the chime in it and the exquisite inner mechanics.

Ibid.

For a while after you quit Keats all other poetry seems to be only whistling or humming.

Ibid.

Dorian Gray is little more than a somewhat highly charged fairy tale which stimulates adolescents to intellectual activity at about seventeen ... It is in the lower ragged edge of 'literature', just as *Gone with the Wind* is in the highest brackets of crowd entertainment.

Ibid., 5 October 1940

I'm finishing my novel [*The Last Tycoon*] ... It will, at any rate, be nothing like anything else as I'm digging it out of myself like uranium – one ounce to the cubic ton of rejected ideas.

Ibid., 23 November 1940

All good writing is *swimming under water* and holding your breath.

Ibid., undated

Read the terrible chapter in *Das Kapital* on 'The Working Day', and see if you are ever quite the same.

Ibid.

So much writing nowadays suffers both from lack of an attitude and from sheer lack of any material, save what is accumulated in a purely social life. The world, as a rule, does not live on beaches and in country clubs.

Ibid.

Pessimism, Madness & Despair

When I hear a man proclaiming himself an 'average, honest, open fellow', I feel pretty sure that he has some definite and perhaps terrible abnormality which he has agreed to conceal.

'The Rich Boy'

All is lost save memory.

'My Lost City'

Sunday – not a day, but rather a gap between two other days.

'Crazy Sunday'

Life was a damned muddle ... a football game with everyone off-side and the referee gotten rid of – everyone claiming the referee would have been on his side.

This Side of Paradise

Happiness ... is only the first hour after the alleviation of some especially intense misery.

The Beautiful and Damned

It is the manner of life seldom to strike but always to wear away.

Ibid.

One of those personalities who, in spite of all their words, are inarticulate, he seemed to have inherited only the vast tradition of human failure – that, and the sense of death.

Ibid.

Routine comes down like twilight on a harsh landscape, softening it until it is tolerable.

Ibid.

Very few of the people who accentuate the futility of life remark the futility of themselves.

Ibid.

'What'll we do with ourselves this afternoon?' cried Daisy, 'and the day after that, and the next thirty years?'
The Great Gatsby

Thirty – the promise of a decade of loneliness, a thinning list of single men to know, a thinning brief-case of enthusiasm, thinning hair.

Ibid.

A sense of the fundamental decencies is parcelled out unequally at birth.

Ibid.

Most affectations conceal something eventually, even though they don't in the beginning.

Ibid.

It is invariably saddening to look through new eyes at things upon which you have expended your own powers of adjustment.

Ibid.

In a real dark night of the soul it is always three o'clock in the morning, day after day.

The Crack-Up

Experience is ... not a thing that happens pleasantly to a passive you – it's a wall that an active you runs up against.

Ibid.

'I used to think until you're eighteen nothing matters,' said Mary.
'That's right,' Abe agreed. 'And afterward it's the same way.'

Tender is the Night

One writes of scars healed, a loose parallel to the pathology of the skin, but there is no such thing in the life of an individual. There are open wounds, shrunk sometimes to the size of a pin-prick but wounds still. The marks of suffering are more comparable to the loss of a finger, or of the sight of an eye. We may not miss them, either, for one minute in a year, but if we should there is nothing to be done about it.

Ibid.

My politeness is a trick of the heart.

Ibid.

The brilliance, the versatility of madness is akin to the resourcefulness of water seeping through, over and around a dike.

Ibid.

Being alone in body and spirit begets loneliness, and loneliness begets more loneliness.

Ibid.

No mature Aryan is able to profit by a humiliation; when he forgives it has become part of his life, he has identified himself with the thing which has humiliated him.

Ibid.

The manner remains intact for some time after the morale cracks.

Ibid.

He found an attitude at length – he was outraged.

The Last Tycoon

One tried anxiously to live in the present – or, if there was no present, to invent one.

Ibid.

Situations where there is no real reason for anything. You pretend there is.

Ibid.

Pessimism, Madness & Despair

Do I look like death? (in mirror at 6 p.m.)

Ibid.

Most of us could be photographed from the day of our birth to the day of our death and the film shown, without producing any emotion except boredom and disgust. It would all just look like monkeys scratching.

Ibid.

Tragedy of these men was that nothing in their lives had really bitten deep.

Ibid.

Not one survived the castration.

Ibid.

To a profound pessimist about life, being in danger is not depressing.

The Letters, 14 November 1917

Italy ... a dead land where everything that could be done or said was done or said long ago – for whoever is deceived by the pseudo-activity under Mussolini is deceived by the spasmodic last jerk of a corpse.

Ibid., 19 April 1925

The insane are always mere guests on earth, eternal strangers carrying around broken decalogues that they cannot read.

Ibid., December 1940

Maxims & Aphorisms

He clung desperately to his rule of never betraying an inferior emotion until he no longer felt it.

'Crazy Sunday'

Don't let the victor belong to the spoils.

The Beautiful and Damned

I can't be bothered resisting things I want. My way is not to want them. *Ibid.*

Let leniency walk in the wake of victory. *Ibid.*

It is the sum of all your judgements that counts.

Ibid.

There's only one lesson to be learned from life ... That there's no lesson to be learned from life. *Ibid.*

Your finger-nails never seem dirty until you wash your hands. *Ibid.*

Reserving judgements is a matter of infinite hope.

The Great Gatsby

Life is much more successfully looked at from a single window, after all. *Ibid.*

The test of a first-rate intelligence is the ability to hold two opposed ideas in the mind at the same time, and still retain the ability to function.

The Crack-Up

Optimism is the content of small men in high places.

Ibid.

Receding from a grief, it seems necessary to retrace the same steps that brought us there. *Tender is the Night*

Sometimes it is harder to deprive oneself of a pain than of a pleasure. *Ibid.*

An indifference cherished, or left to atrophy, becomes an emptiness. *Ibid.*

Nothing was more conducive to the development of observation than compulsory silence. *Ibid.*

In French you can be heroic and gallant with dignity ... But in English you can't be heroic and gallant without being a little absurd. *Ibid.*

It's not a slam at you when people are rude – it's a slam at the people they've met before.

The Last Tycoon

A mixed motive is conspicuous waste. *Ibid.*

There is no substitute for will. Sometimes you have to fake will when you don't feel it at all. *Ibid.*

If you are in a position to give credit to yourself, then you do not need it. *Ibid.*

The cleverly expressed opposite of any generally accepted idea is worth a fortune to somebody. *Ibid.*

We never quite understand each other and perhaps that's the best basis for an enduring friendship.
The Letters, c. March 1933

Nobody *naturally* likes a mind quicker than their own.
Ibid., 8 August 1933

Most of the great things you learn in life are in periods of enforced silence. *Ibid.*

Popularity is not worth a damn and respect is worth everything, and what do you care about happiness – and who does except the perpetual children of this world?
Ibid.

At 40 one counts carefully one's remaining vitality and resources.

Ibid., February 1937

For premature adventure one pays an atrocious price.
Ibid., 5 July 1937

Whatever your sins are I hope you never get to justify them to yourself.

Ibid.

There is no other time but now.
Ibid., 8 October 1937

She realized too late that work was dignity, and the only dignity.

Ibid., 7 July 1938

Nothing is so obnoxious as other people's luck.
Ibid., 19 September 1938

Be a little penurious with your small change.
Ibid., March 1939

You cannot imitate a mannerism with profit.
Ibid., 9 August 1939

The pith of my advice is: think what you want, the less said the better.

Ibid., 15 March 1940

The ends will take care of themselves.
Ibid., 5 September 1940

No possible triumph is worth the loss of your health.
Ibid., 17 September 1940

You must have some politeness towards ideas.
Ibid., undated